Love

Valentine's Day Coloring Book

Ayn Eliot

Happy Coloring

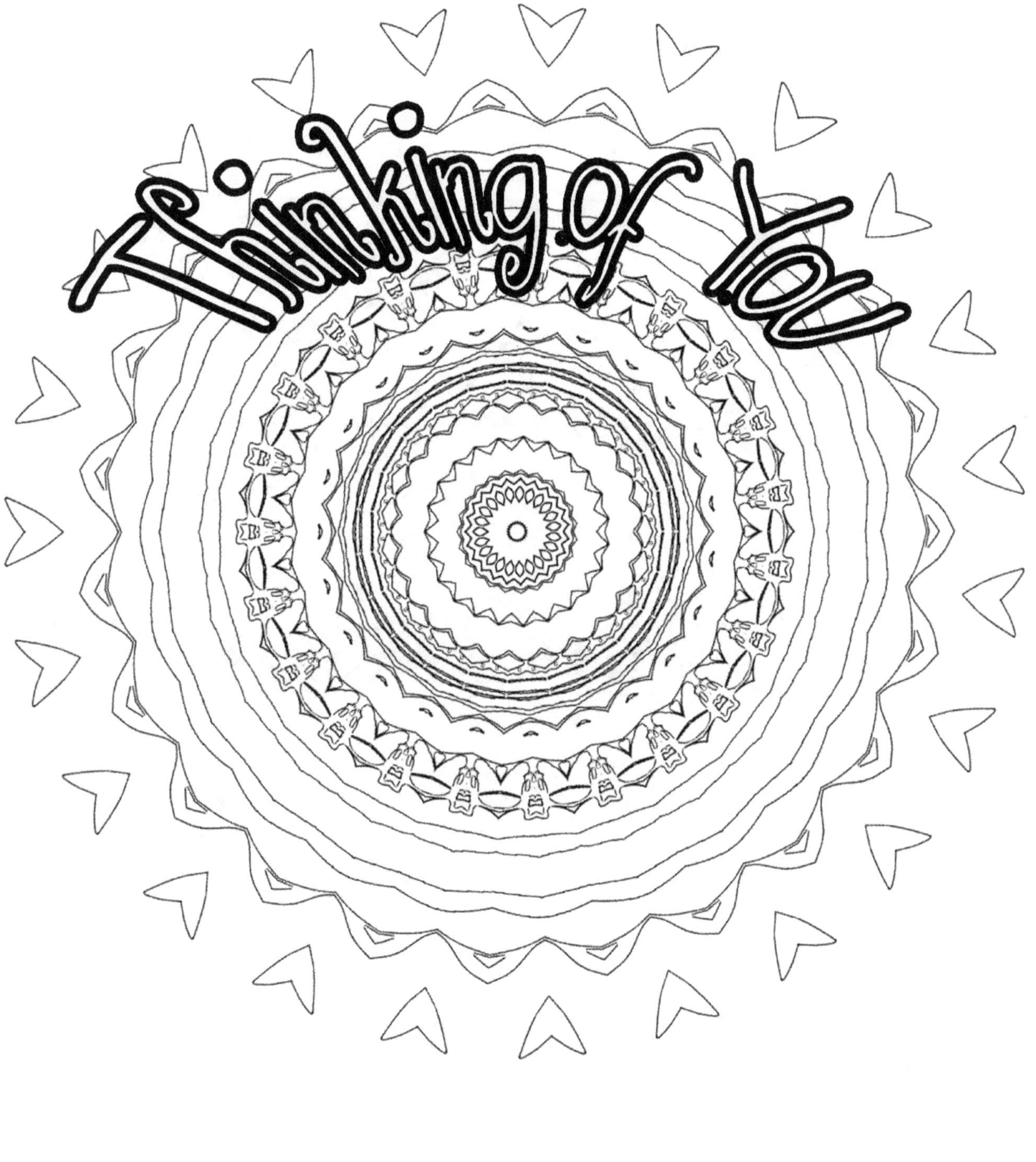
Thinking of You

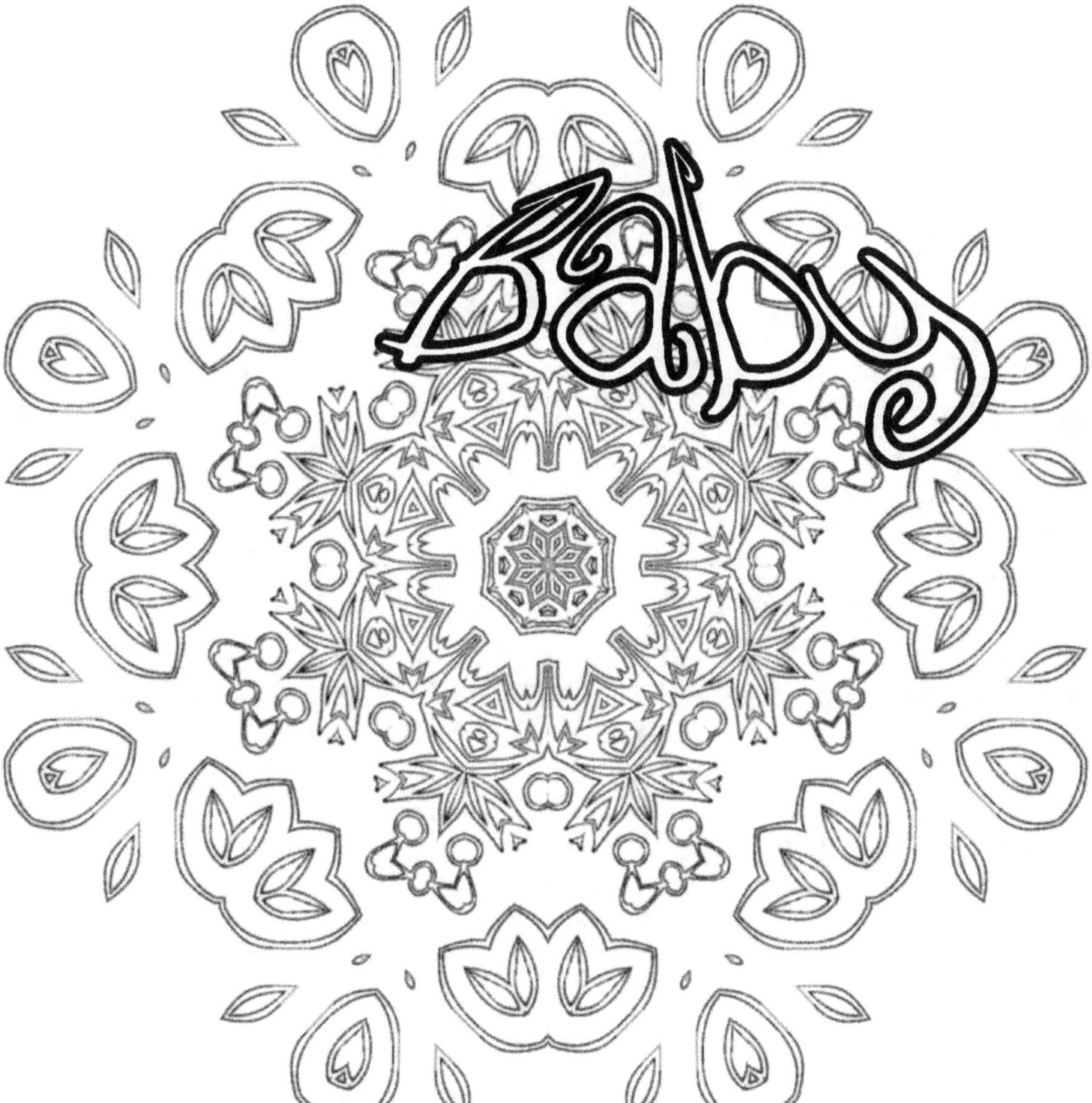
Baby

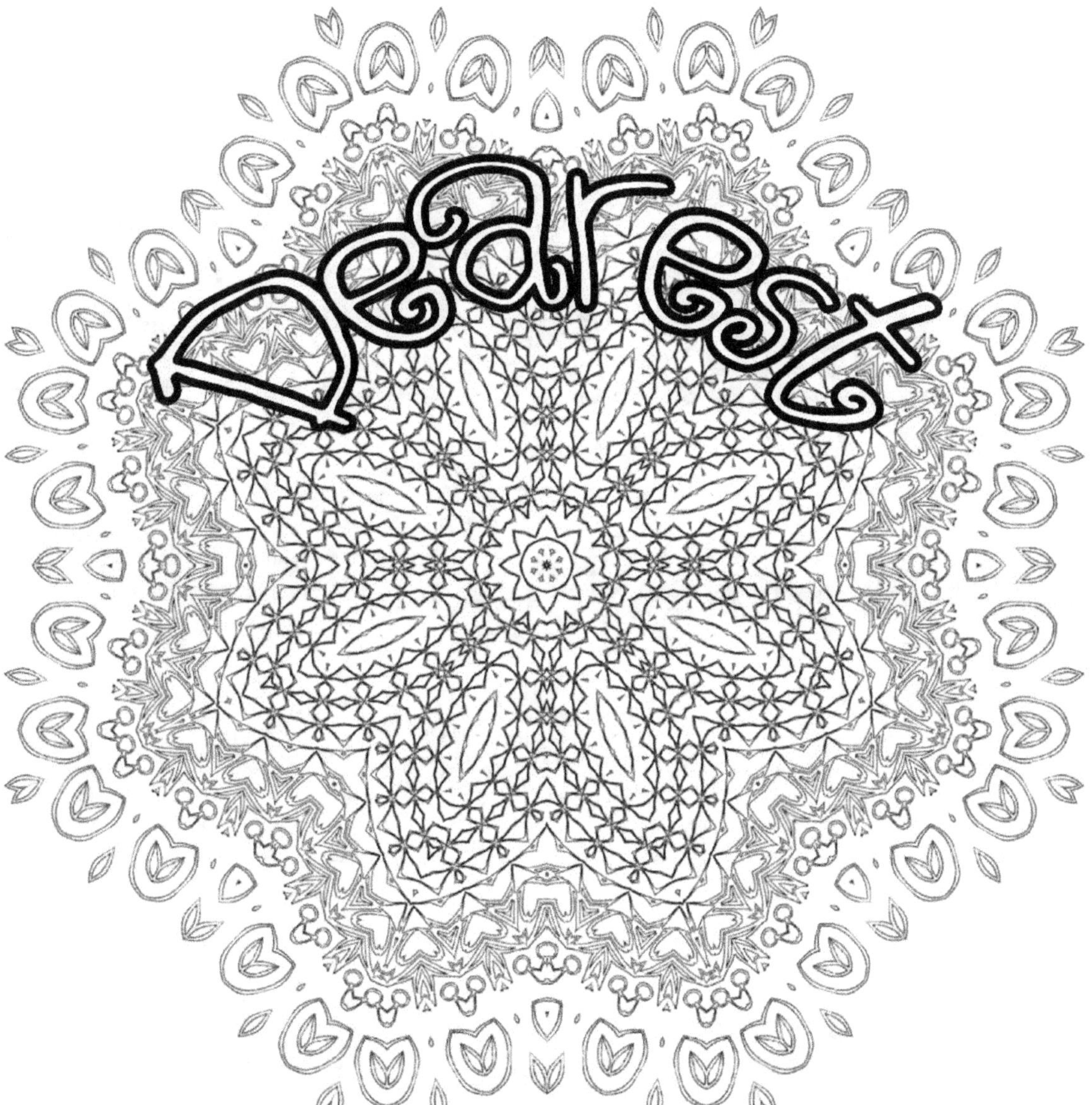
Dearest

love is like a dream

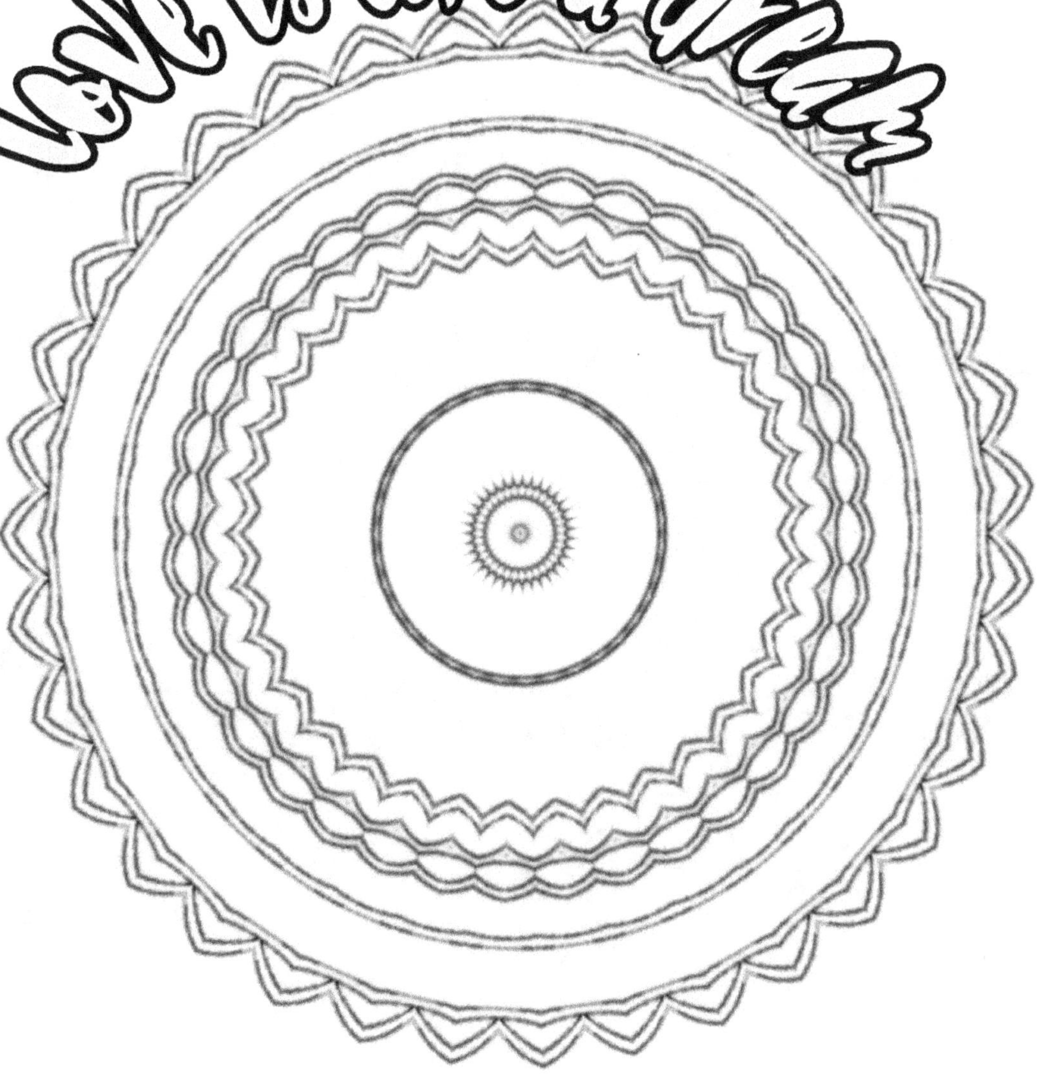

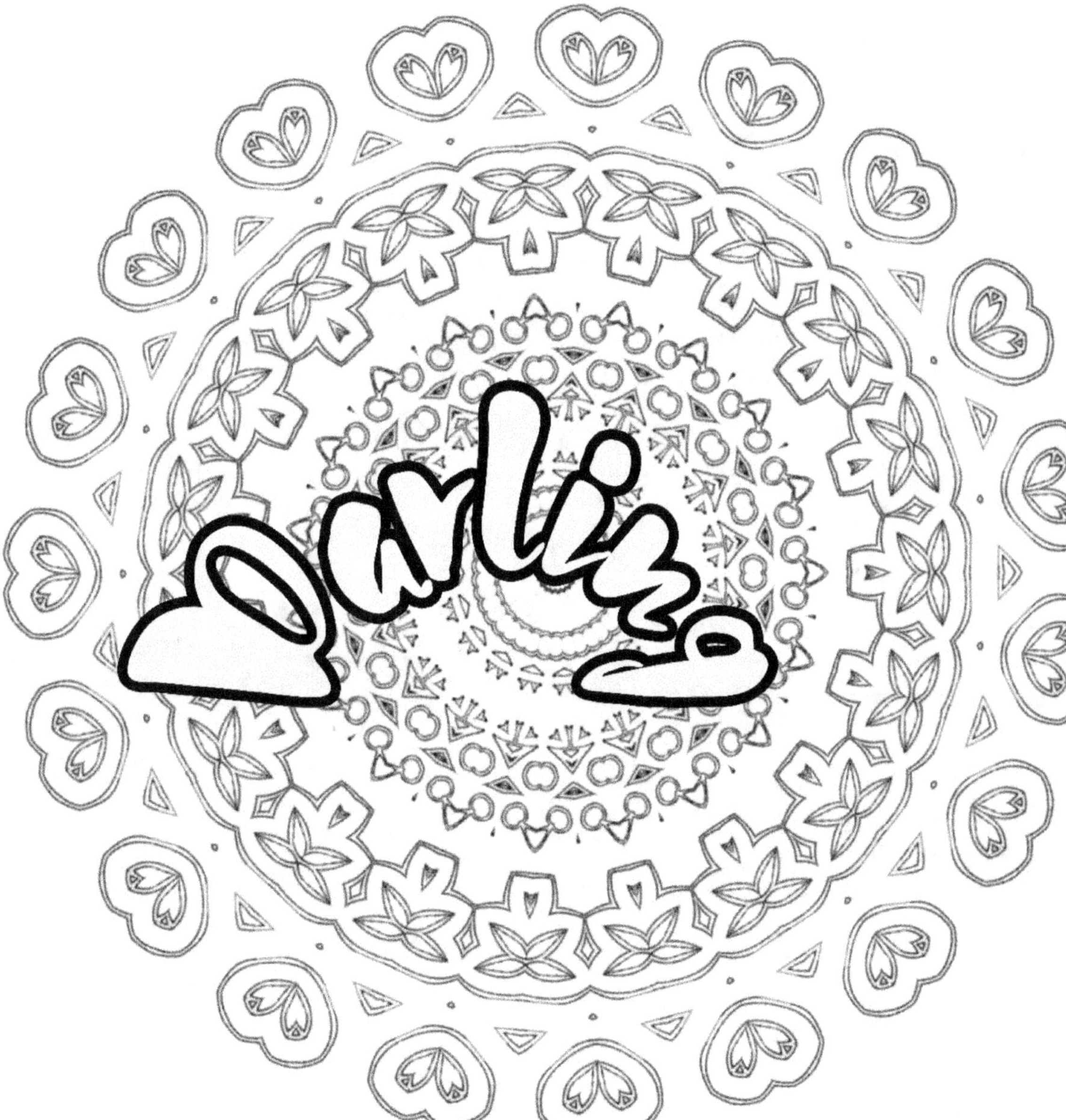
Darling

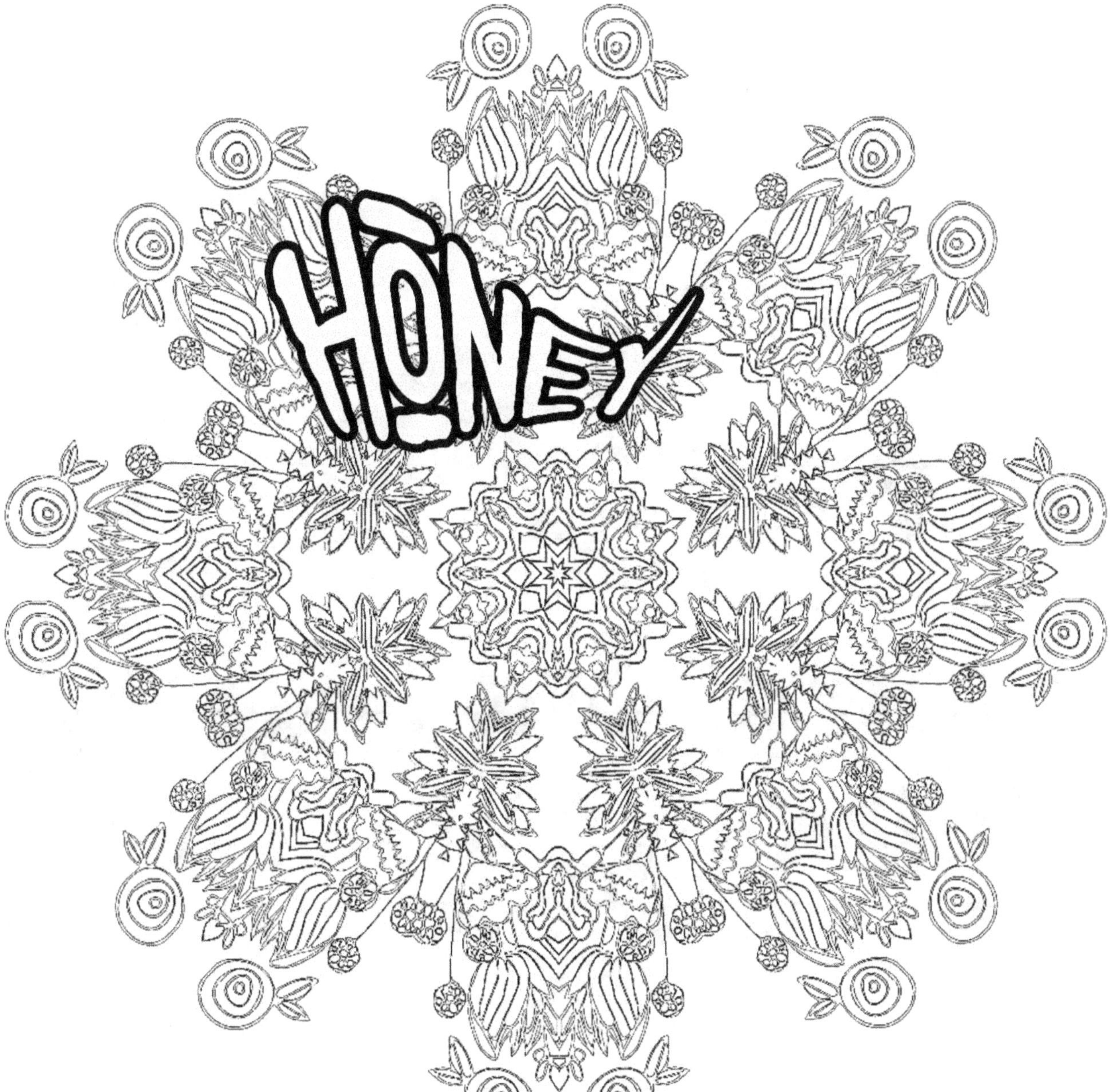
HONEY

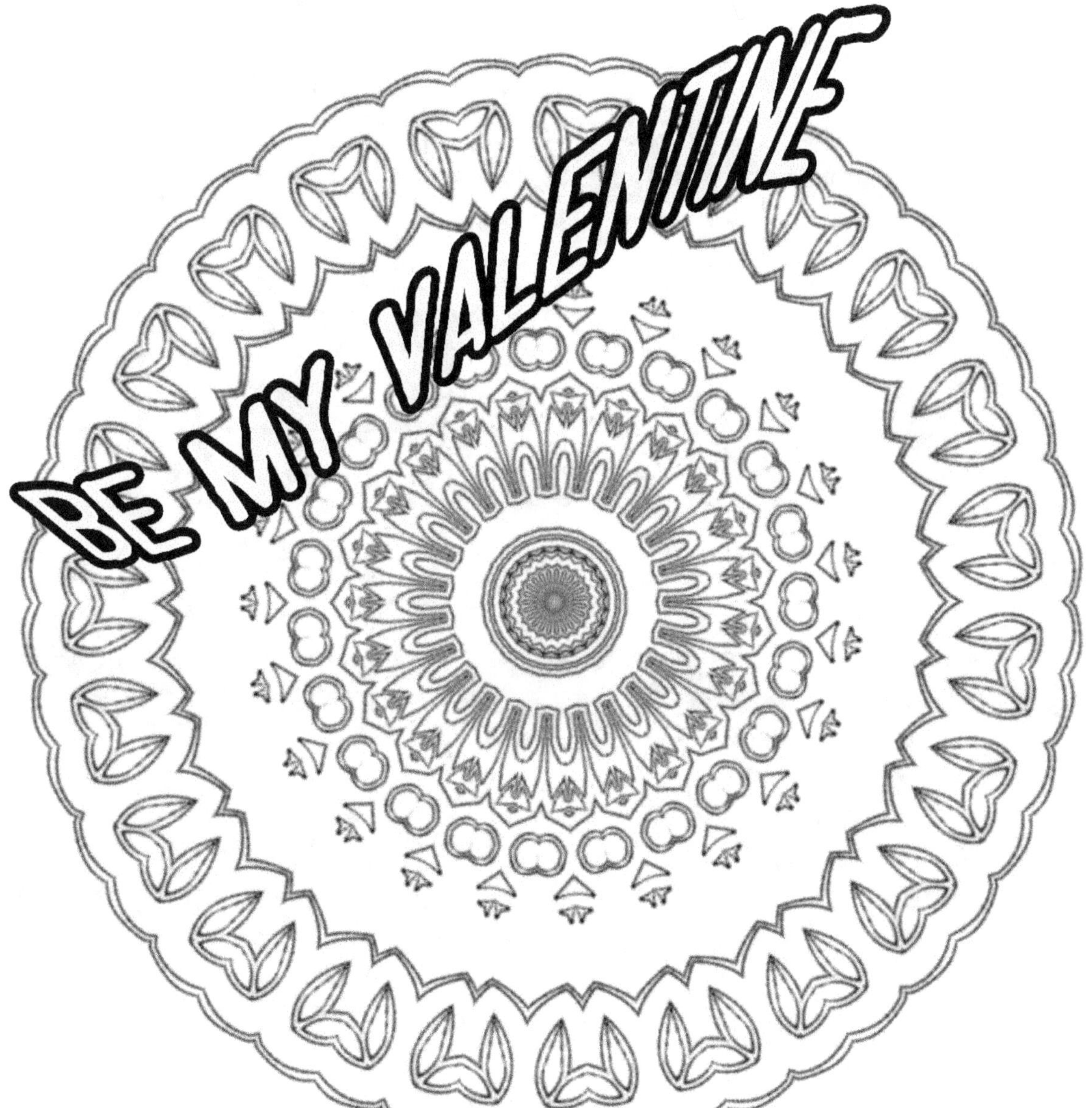
BE MY VALENTINE

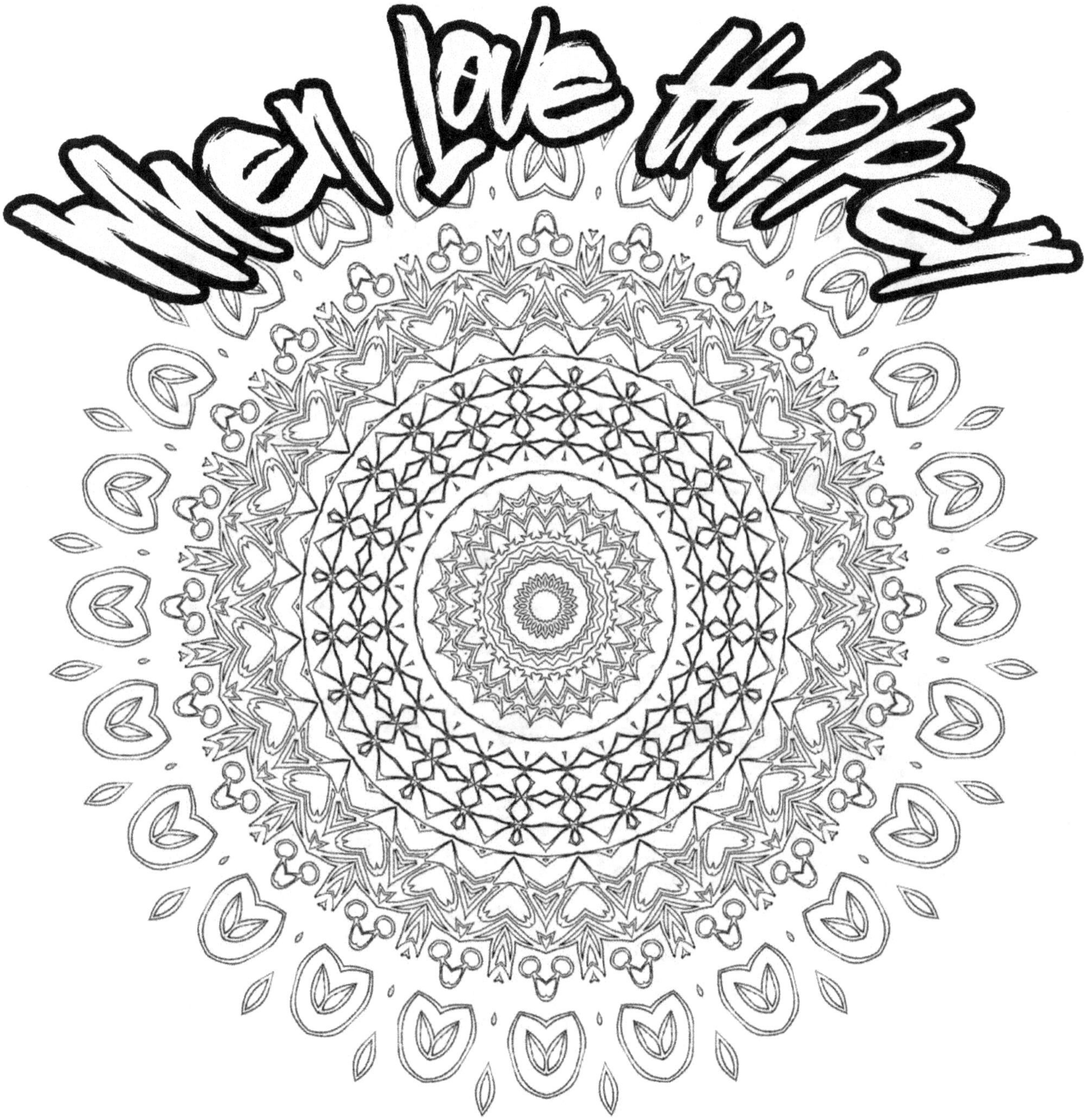
When Love Happen

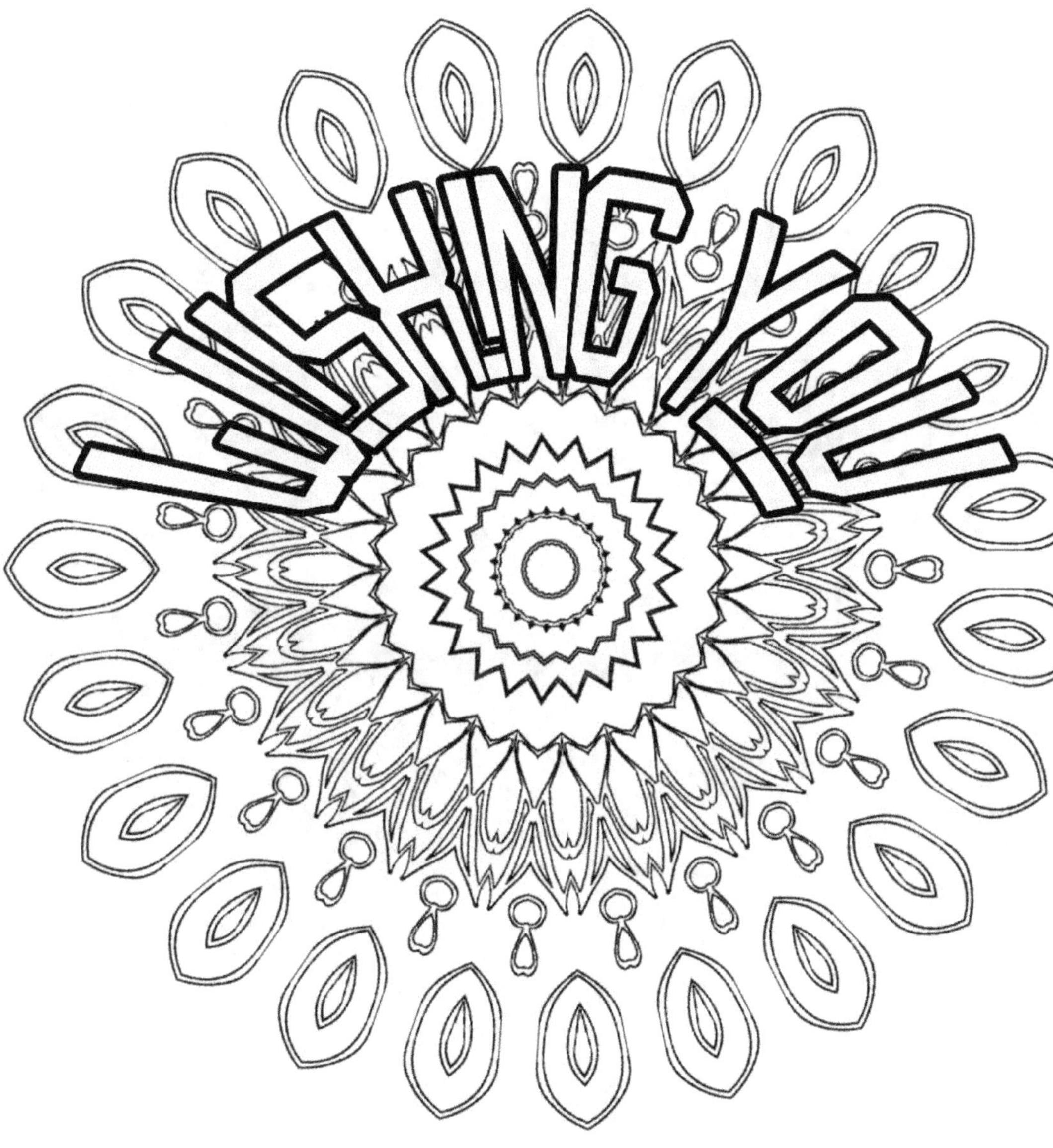
WISHING YOU

Honeybunch

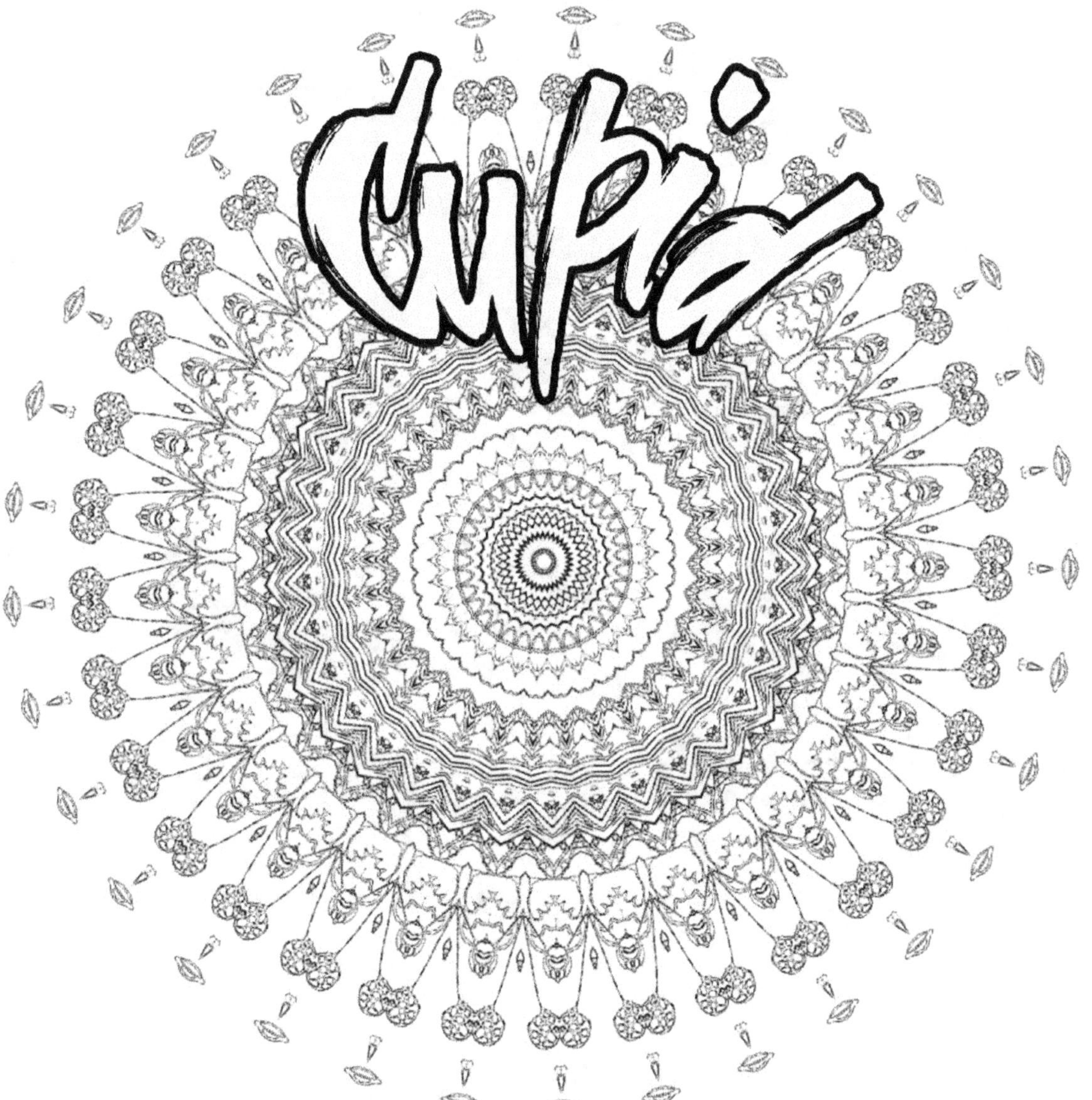
cupid

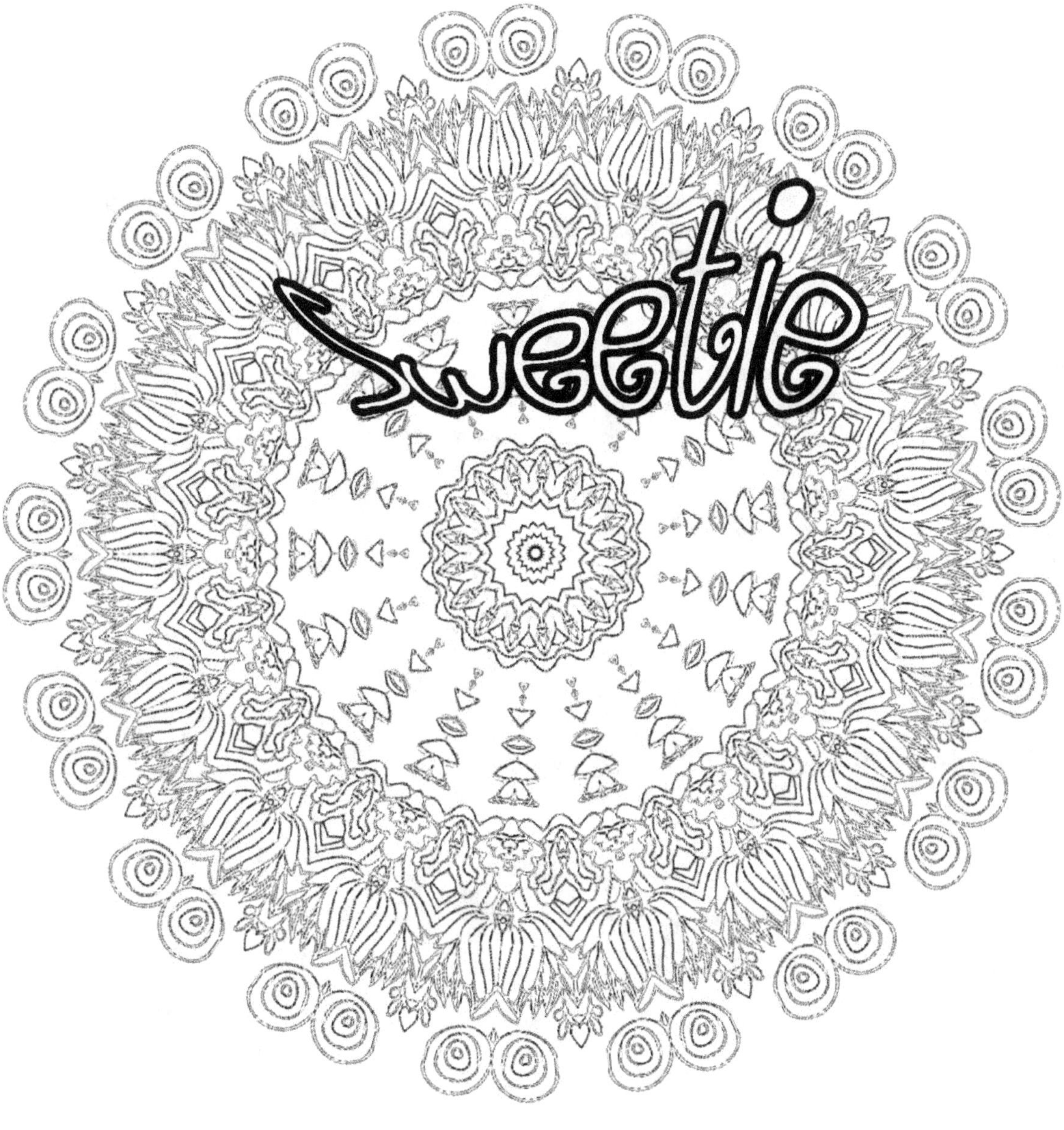
Sweetie

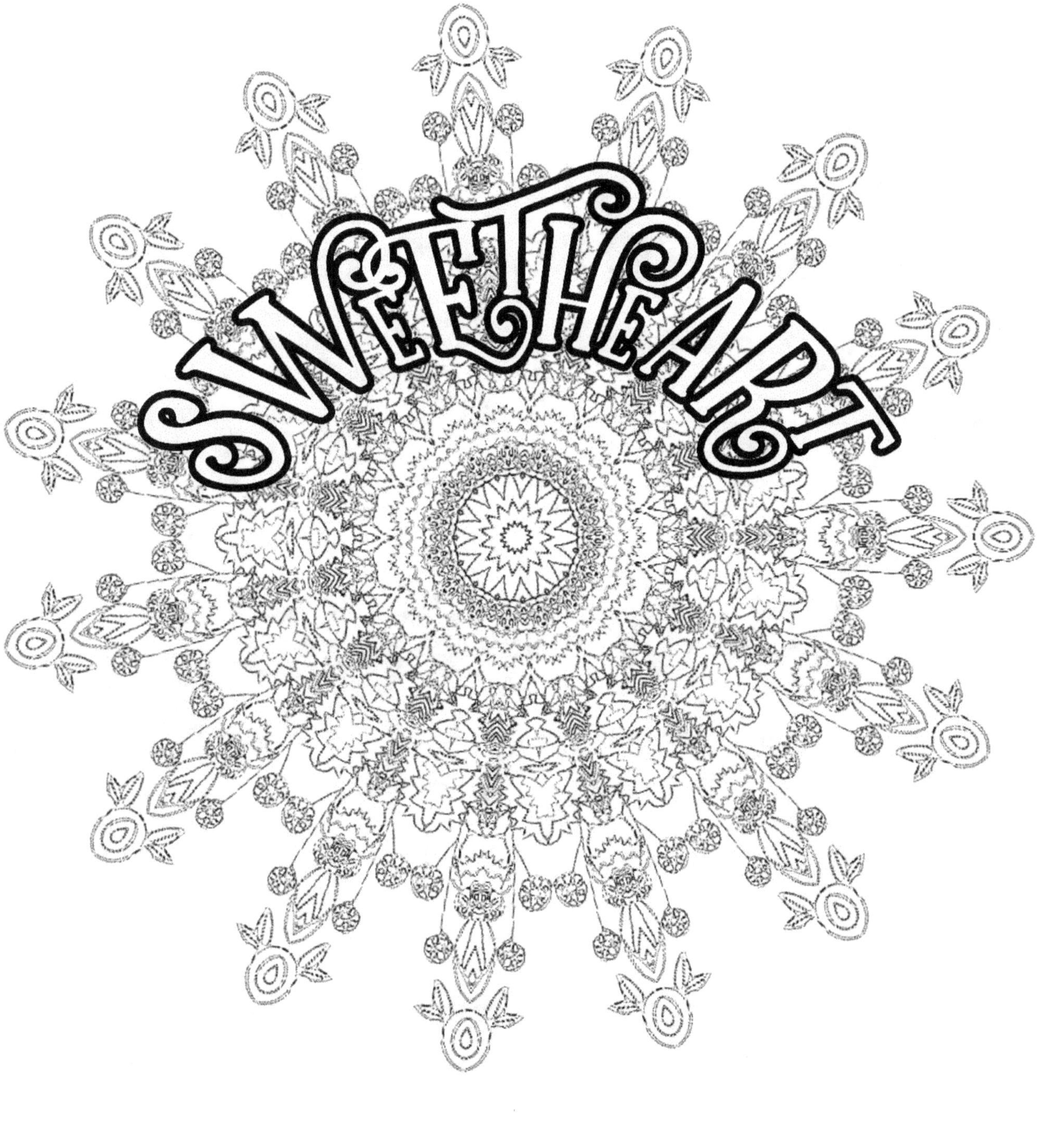
SWEETHEART

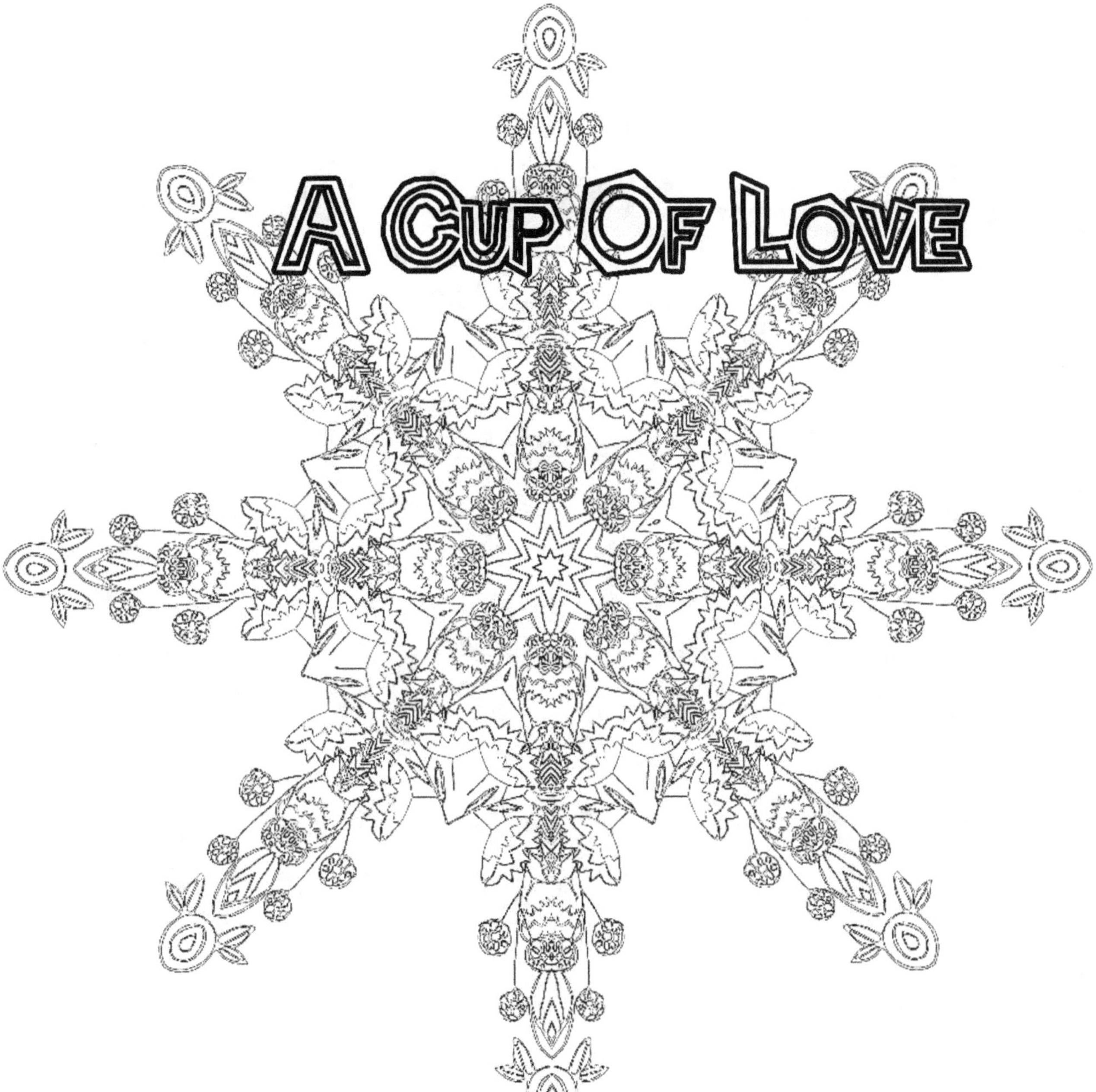
A Cup Of Love

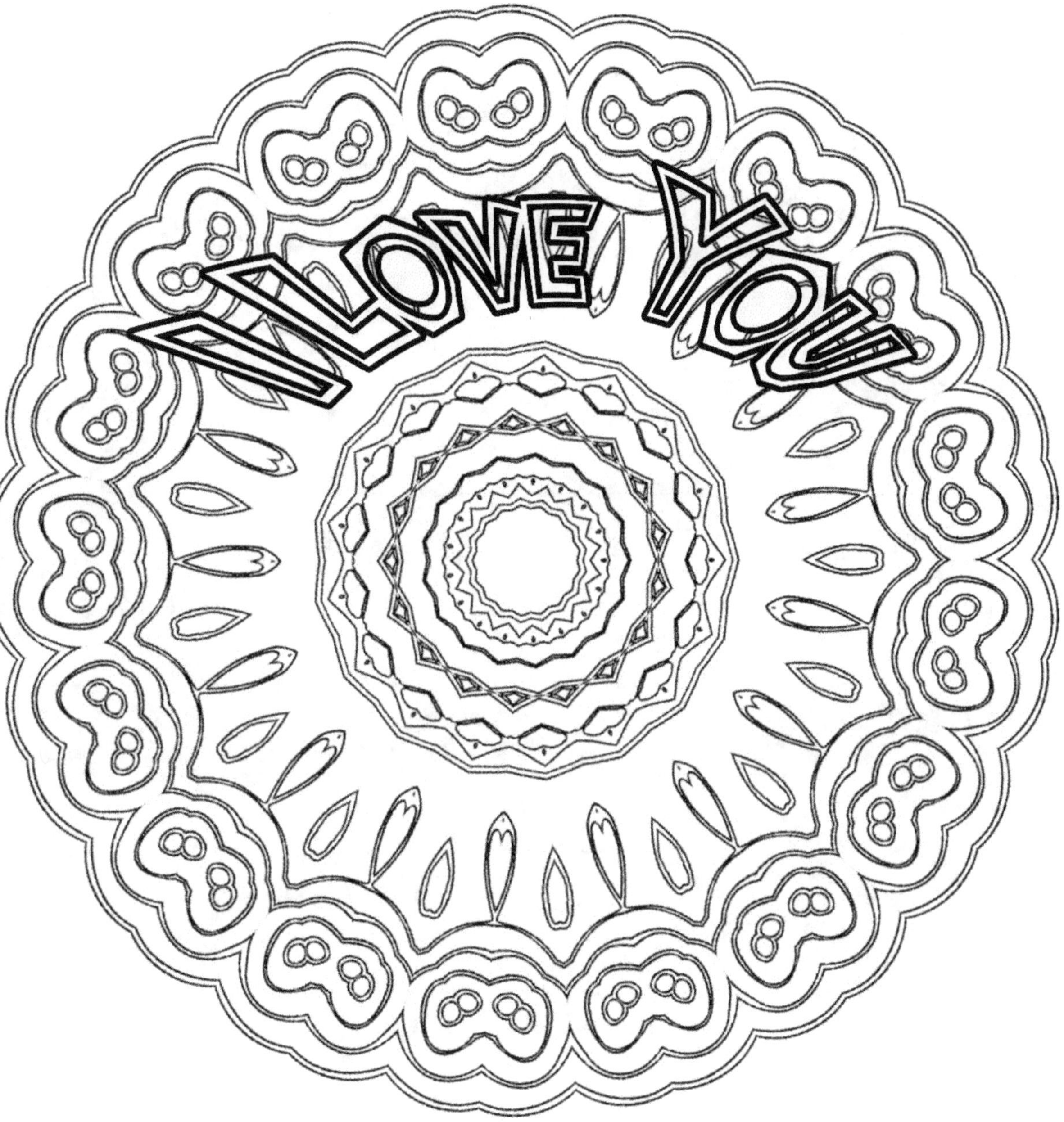
I LOVE YOU

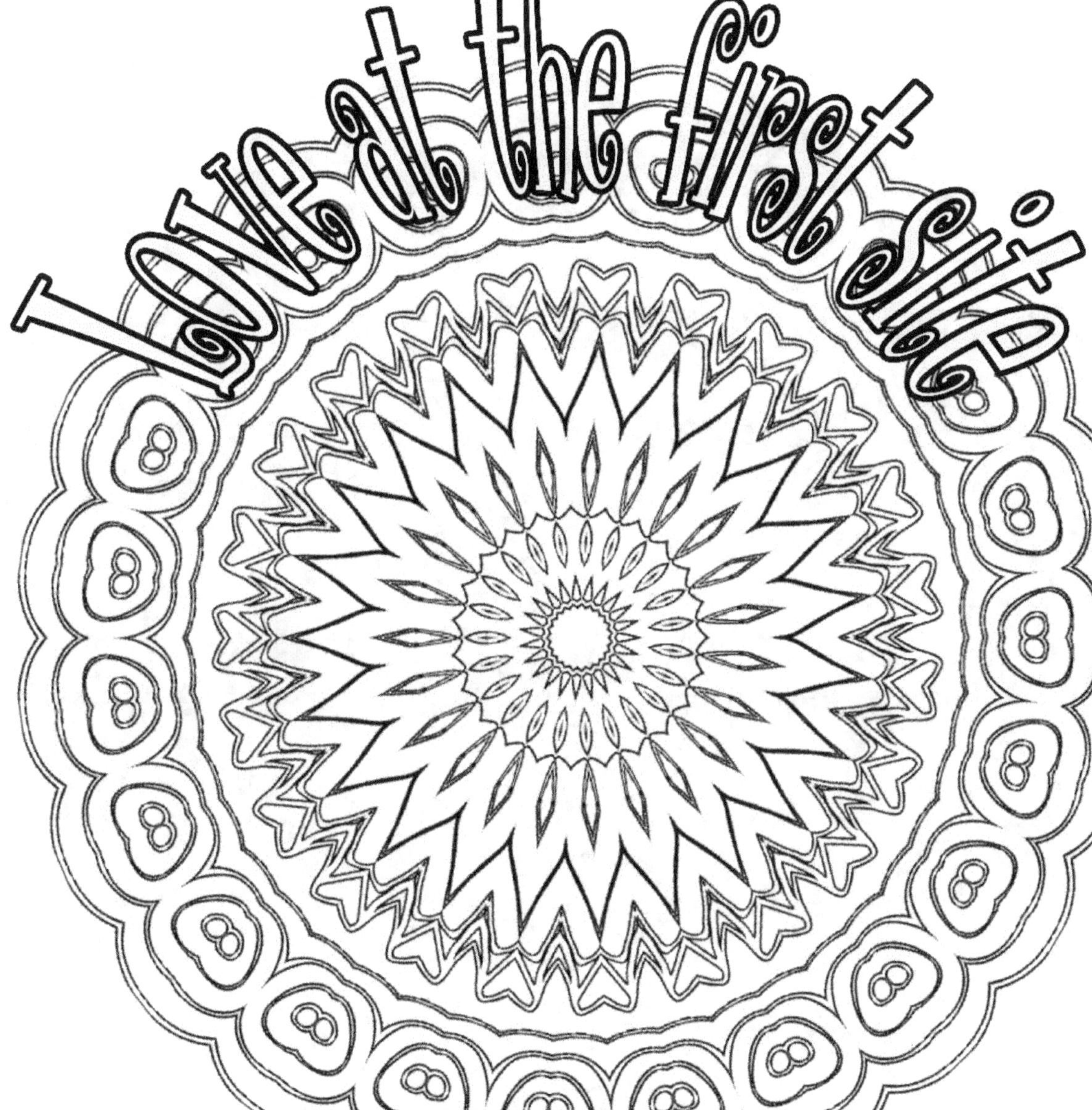
Love at the first site

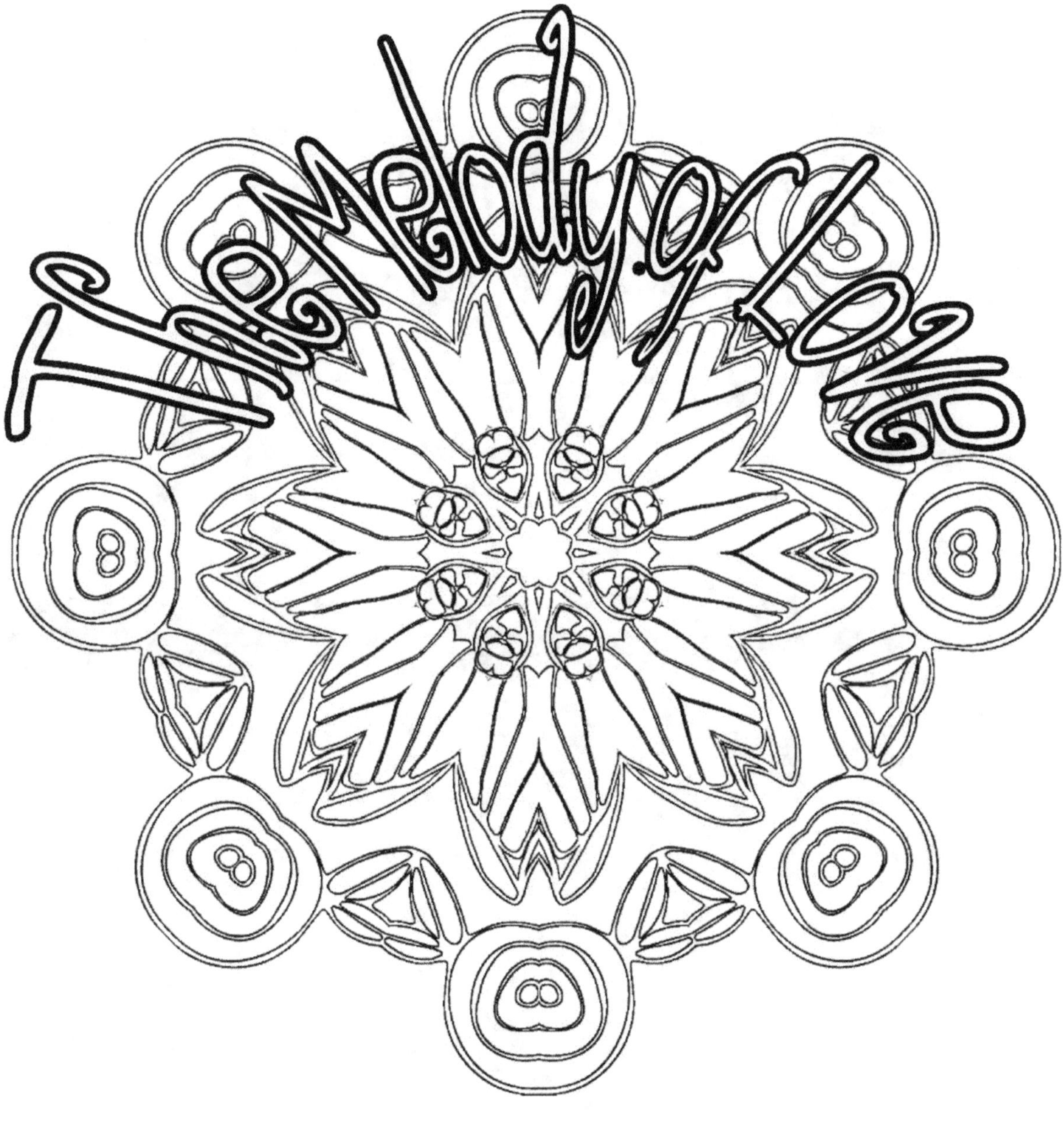
The Melody of Love

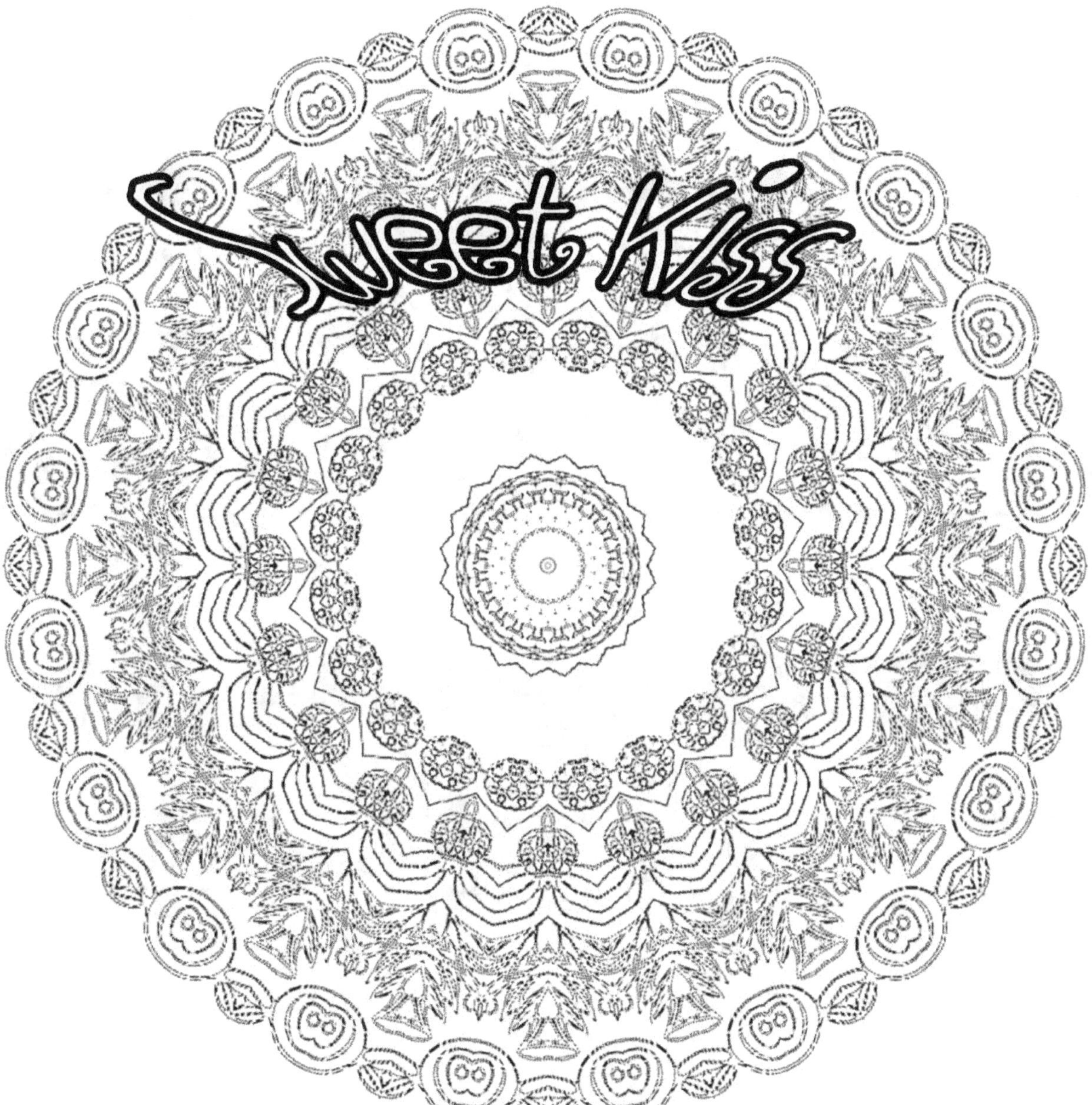
Sweet Kiss

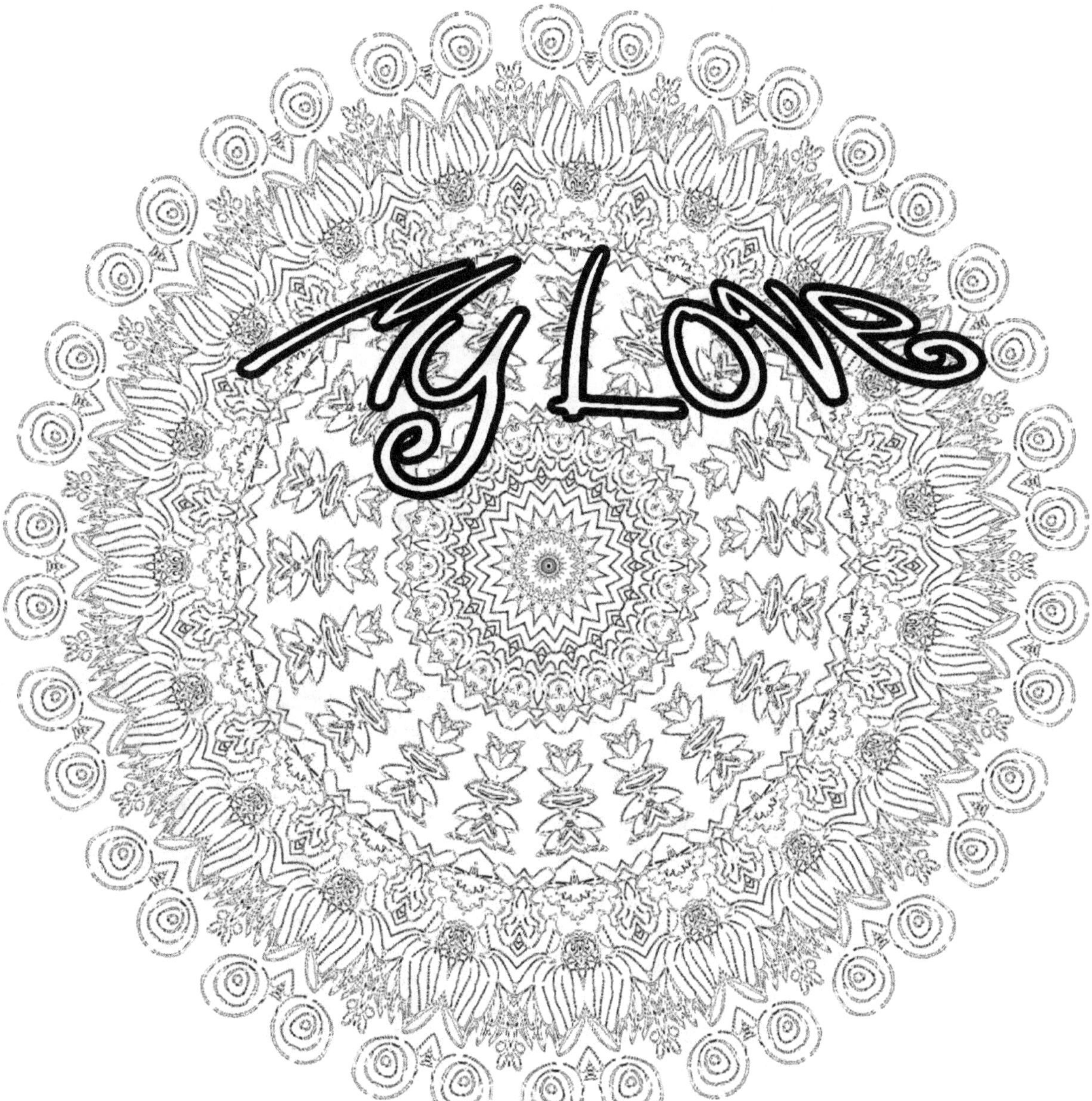
My Love

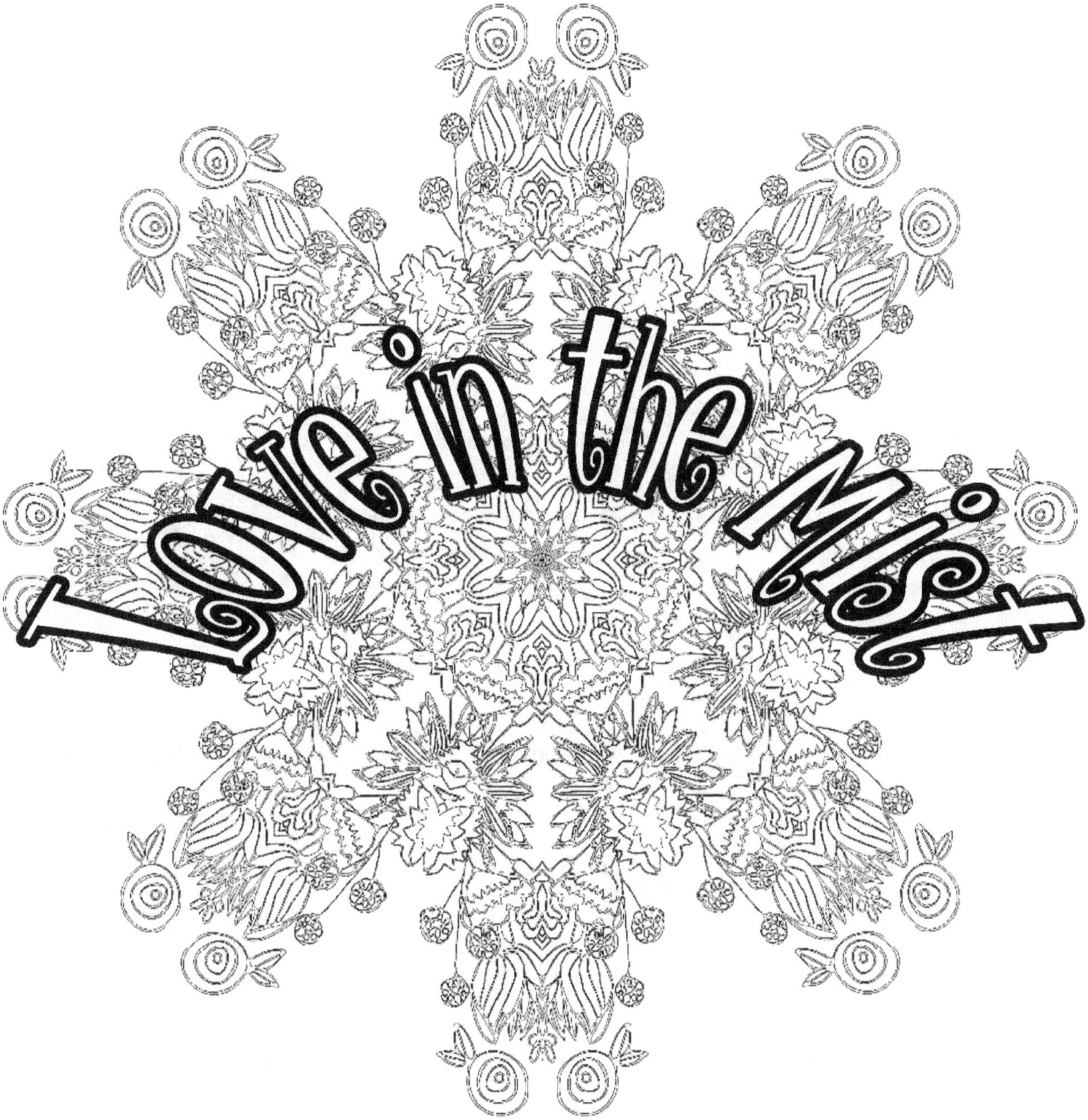
Love in the Mist

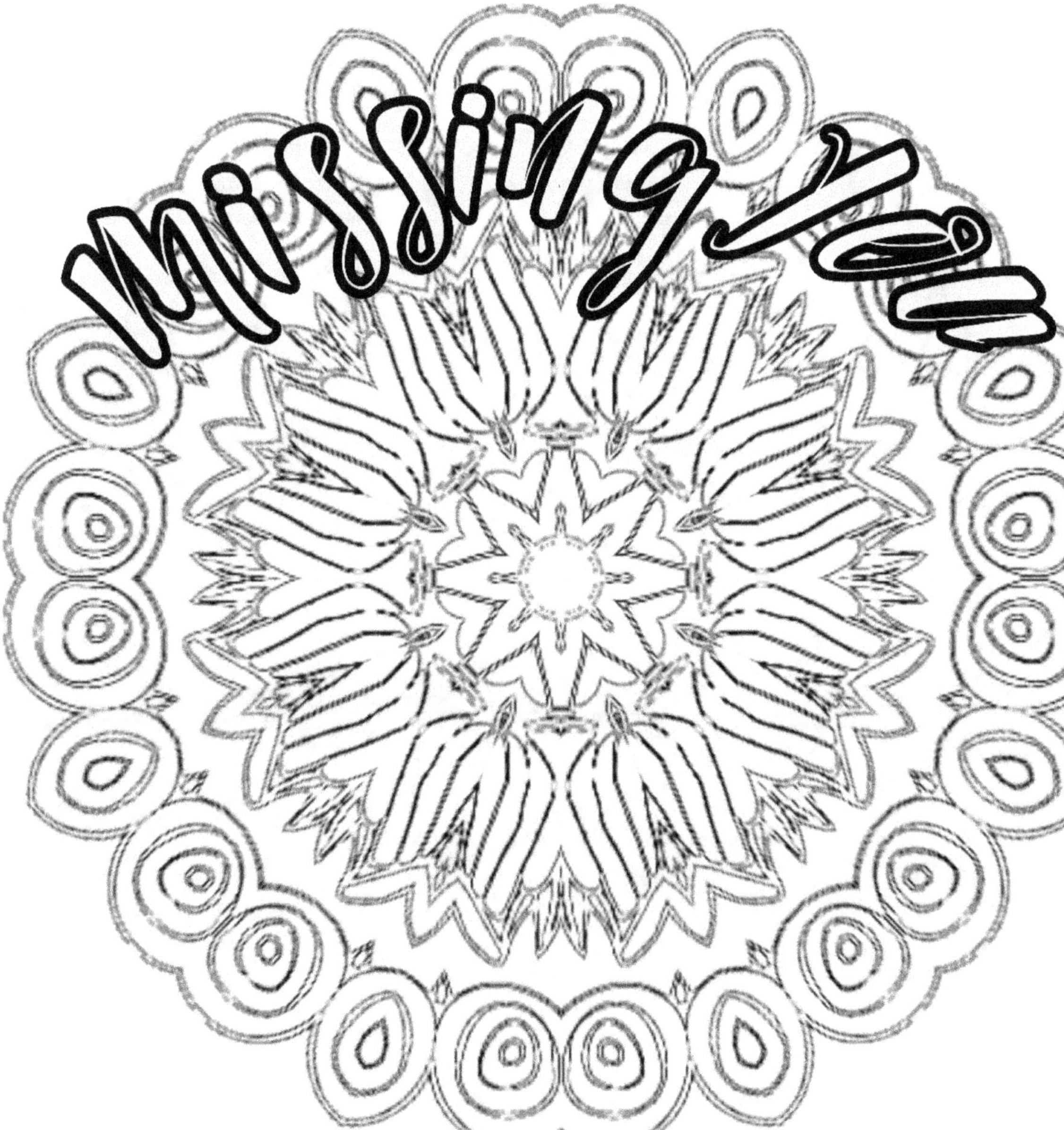
Missing You

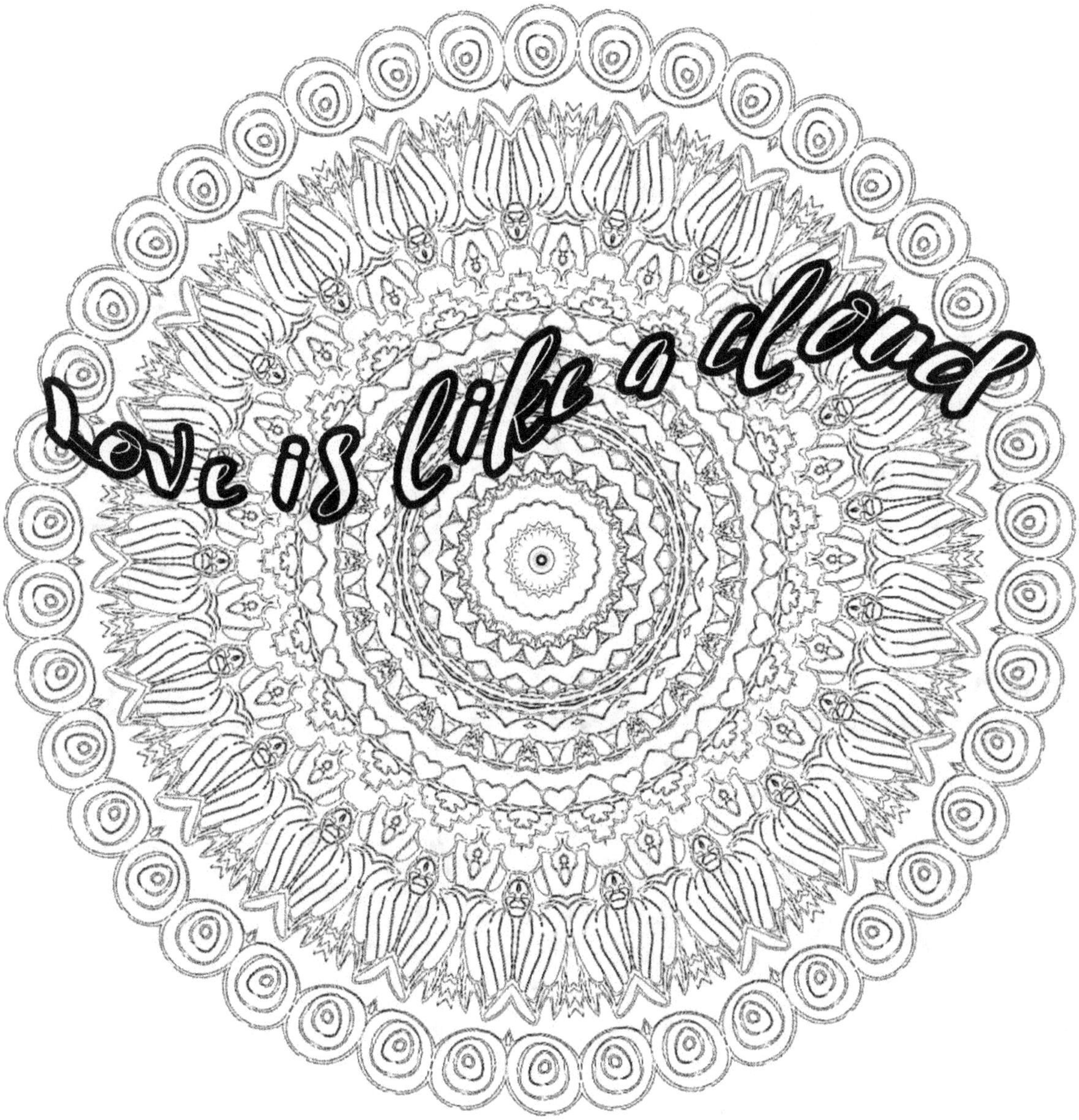
Love is like a cloud

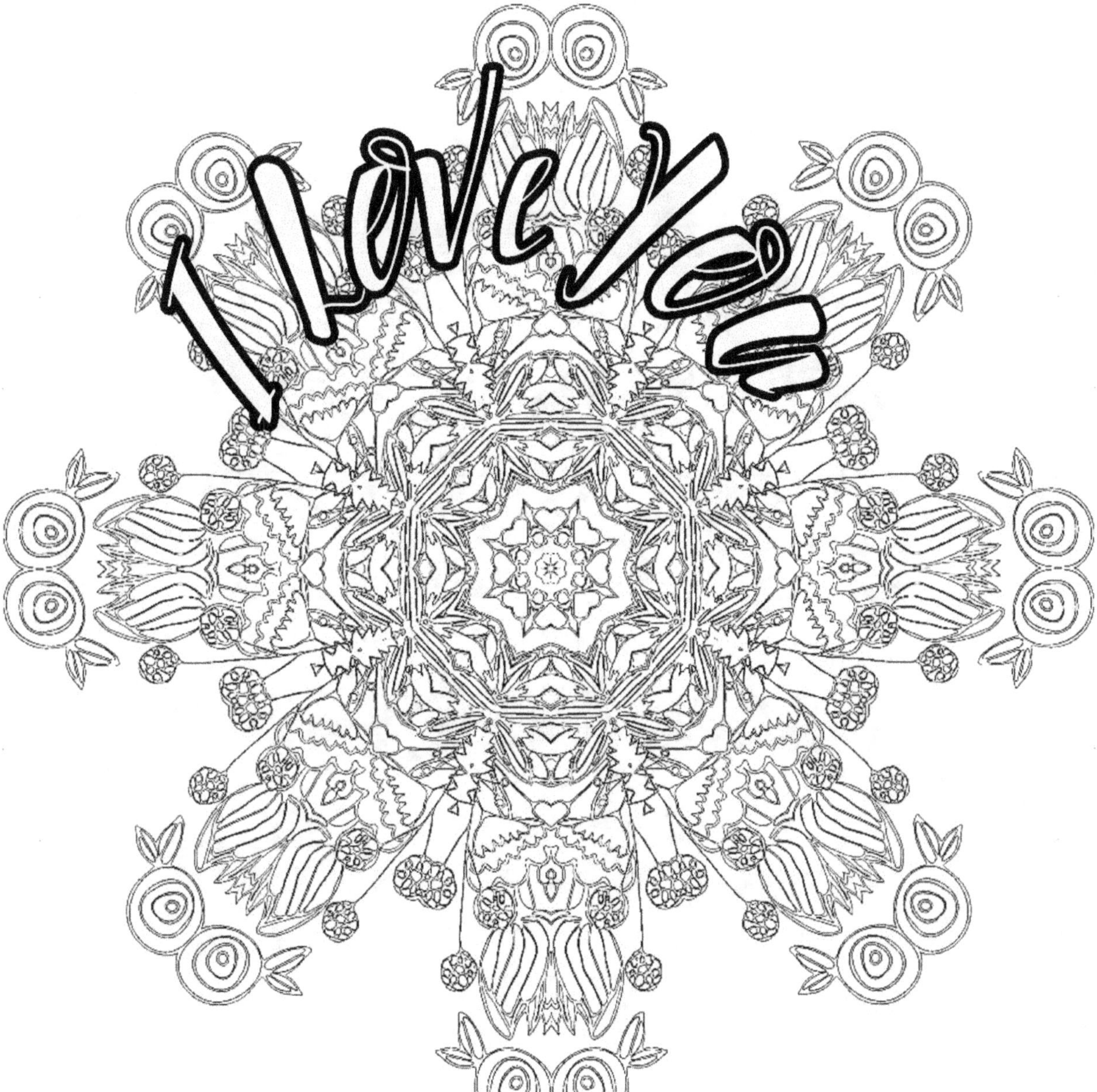
I Love You

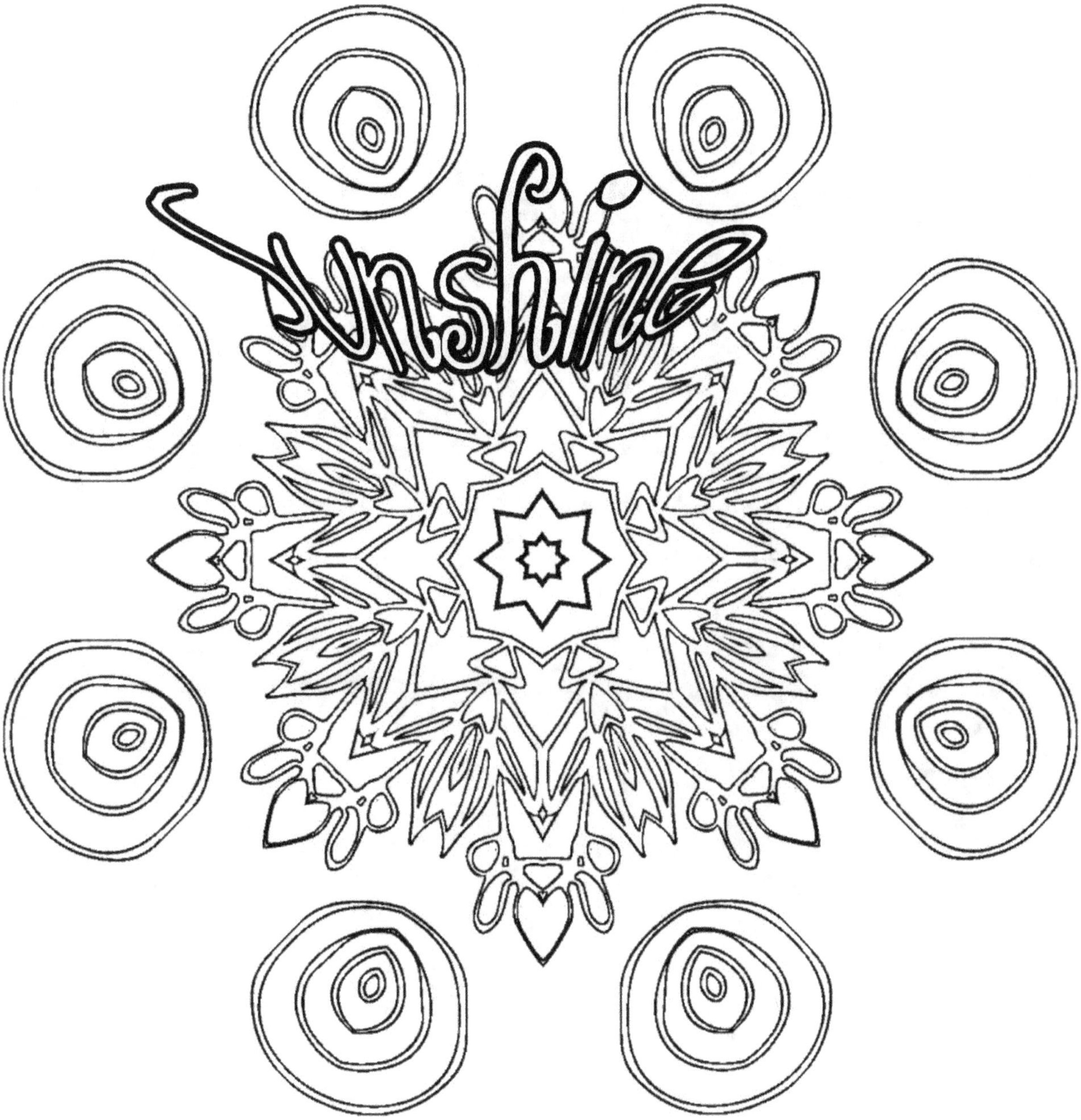
Sunshine

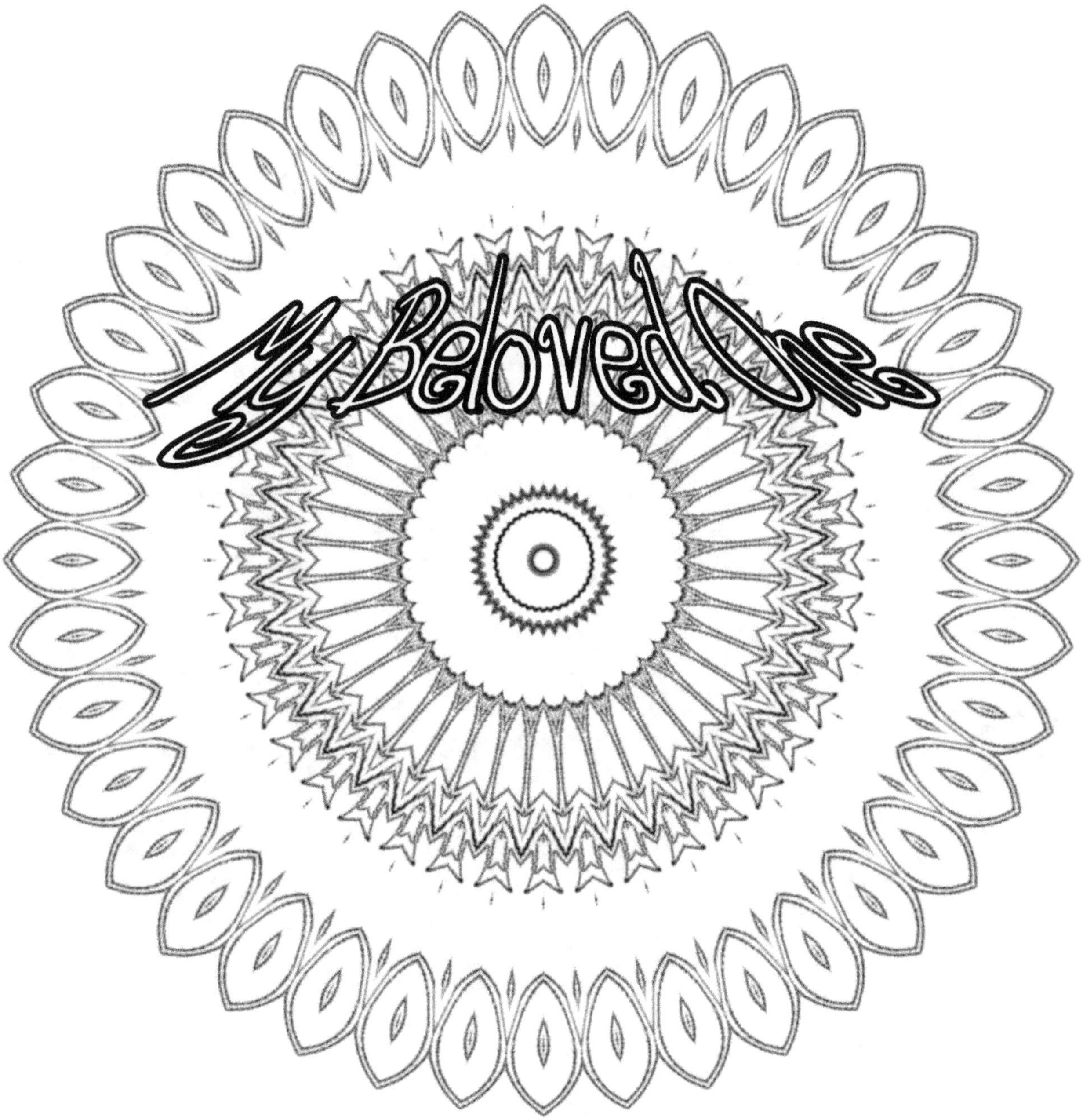
My Beloved One

www.ingramcontent.com/pod-product-compliance
Lightning Source LLC
Chambersburg PA
CBHW081749170526
45167CB00009B/3977
* 9 7 8 1 5 4 3 0 4 5 2 1 5 *